1

Invisible Voices

Dreaming
Invisible Voices

Poetry by James McGrath
Drawings by Margreta Overbeck

Sunstone
Press

SANTA FE

Cover and all drawings by Margreta Overbeck

Sunstone books may be purchased for educational, business, or sales promotional use.
For information please write: Special Markets Department, Sunstone Press,
P.O. Box 2321, Santa Fe, New Mexico 87504-2321.

Book design › Vicki Ahl
Body typeface › Benjamin
Printed on acid free paper

Library of Congress Cataloging-in-Publication Data

McGrath, James, 1928-
    Dreaming invisible voices : poems / James McGrath ; drawings, Margreta Overbeck ;
cover and all drawings by Margreta Overbeck.
        p. cm.
    ISBN 978-0-86534-713-7 (softcover : alk. paper)
    I. Title.
    PS3613.C497D74 2009
    811'.6--dc22
                                    2009002941

WWW.SUNSTONEPRESS.COM
SUNSTONE PRESS / POST OFFICE BOX 2321 / SANTA FE, NM 87504-2321 /USA
(505) 988-4418 / ORDERS ONLY (800) 243-5644 / FAX (505) 988-1025

Contents

Ant to Dog

Elephant
to Ladybug

Lion to Seal

Sea Shell to
Who Walks Beside You?

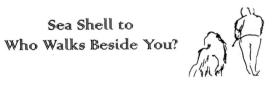

Preface

About the Book, The Artist, and the Poet

The poems in this book began as a response to the animals in the Asian Zodiac Calendar while I was living and working in Japan, Korea, Taiwan, Okinawa, and the Philippines in the 1970s. Other poems written at this time reflected my childhood growing up in Western Washington State in the natural world of rivers, mountains, and wildlife. I put the collection aside for several years.

I met Margreta Overbeck in my art class at the Ponce de Leon Retirement Center in Santa Fe in the 1990s. She gave me all her sketchbooks, created over many years. What an honor!

When I looked through her work I was astonished to find that a number of her drawings illustrated poems that I had written twenty-five years before—a serendipitous coming together of artist and poet.

Margreta was born in 1909 and grew up in the mountains of Glenwood Springs, Colorado, surrounded by creatures from mountain lions to hummingbirds and butterflies.

She related: "My mother taught me to observe nature thoroughly. In high school I had a great teacher, Helen Perry, who was a pupil of André L'Hote. I learned cubism; this was a turning point for me. I got into stained glass, training at the Lamb Studio in New York

City and later made windows for many churches, mostly in Dixieland and the Great Lakes Region as well as New York and Maine. I assisted in creating the stained glass windows in our National Cathedral in Washington, DC. In New Mexico, the First Methodist Church in Albuquerque has my stained glass windows. My art activities have kept me going in my nineties."

Margreta died in Santa Fe, New Mexico, in June 2007 at the age of 97. Her spirit lives on in the beauty she created.

—James McGrath
Santa Fe, New Mexico

Dedication

We dedicate this book to the memory of
our Mothers,
who shared the voices and living things in
the Garden:

Georgia Pratt Overbeck   1887–1955
Millie Mae Norman McGrath   1905–1998

Foreword

Poet James McGrath has given us the gift of enchantment and marvel in this collection Dreaming Invisible Voices. James McGrath takes us to a world filled with magic and prophecy. More so, to the world of flowers, wind, seashells, horses, crickets, caterpillars, and so many other creatures of our Planet that we often fail to see, such as ants and bees and bears.

James McGrath has the talent of a wise and well-crafted poet but also a poet of empathy and compassion allowing us, the readers, to hear the sentiment of living things this poet sings about. Each poem, written in the first person, allows us to imagine what it is like to be a cloud or a caterpillar or the scent of a flower.

With a passionate imagination and the innocence of a magnificent poet, James McGrath gently takes us by the hand and guides us to what is often invisible to the eye but not the soul, as Antoine de Saint Exupery states in *The Little Prince*.

These poems must be read slowly, perhaps in a quiet day of winter or in the plenitude of summer as they are filled with enchantment and at the same time with tenderness. Often. These poems can be read as treaties on Human Rights and the protection of the environment.

I am moved by these poems that embrace the earth, the cloud, the family of animals and humans engaged in the practice of true humanity, which is also the practice of love and beauty.

James McGrath has given us a splendid gift with splendid illustrations from his artist-collaborator Margreta Overbeck. It's as if Margreta has distilled her over-ninety years of a love affair with the natural world into drawings of simplicity and an inner vision of those Invisible Voices in these poems. This is a collection that celebrates all living things like a prayer in the wind.

—Marjorie Agosin
Wellesley, Massachusetts

To the Human

You are the human.

Each and every space
      between the breathings of time
      is a mirror for you,

      a bright window to examine, polish,
      shatter, to love what you see.

It is time for you to share
      the light that enters your soul.

That is your reflection.

Ant to Dog

A star fell into the river.
A thousand jays flew up, all of them wanting me.

—Catherine Ferguson,
from "Desire," *The Sound a Raven Makes*

Ant

I have a very great family.

We are everywhere,
      places you will never go,
      under rocks,
      in tree barks,
      holes in the ground,
      behind your refrigerator and bathtub.

We like secret places
      because we have much work to do
      and do not want to be disturbed.

If you watch us,
      you will learn how to share
      when you work.

Some of us carry things,
      some of us store foods,
      some of us make trails
      for others to walk in safety.

And when it is cold
      we gather together
      in our home.
      No one, not even snowflakes,
      will know where we are.

Bear

I am the fur-covered stone in the mountain.

I am the most human of all forest creatures.

I stand upright on two legs
      to greet you.

You have made rugs and coats of my skin.

For that I am sad.

You have put me behind bars in your zoos.

For that I am sad.

I only ask you to listen to me closely.
      I have old legends to tell you.

If you look into the dark sky
      late at night,
      you will see me made of stars.

For that I am happy.

Beaver

I do not eat the tree I cut down.

I build my home of trees.

I use only enough trees
      for a simple home
      in a mountain stream.

If you watch me,
      I will show you
      how to make a dam
      to create a lake
      for frogs, cattails,
      mountain vegetables,
      a playground for fish and wild ducks.

If you watch me,
      I will show you
      how to make a pond
      to catch the moon to write your poems.

Bee

Perhaps
        my life is as blessed
        as yours.

I keep the flowers alive.

I help fruit sweeten the world.

I create the most succulent
        food on earth.

When I work, I waggle-dance and sing.

Perhaps
        my life is as blessed
        as yours.

You receive the scent of flowers.

You have the sweetness of fruit.

You eat the gold of honey
        and when you work in joy
        you can create songs and dances.

Perhaps
        you and I are both blessed.

Bird

— in memory of my flicker Flicka

The clouds are my family.

When you cannot find me,
        it is because my sisters
        and brothers have called me.

We are singing circles of prayers
        about the earth.

I shall build a nest for you
        to rest in.

It will be soft and half-round
        like the moon in your spirit.

Please come to the nest
        I build for you.

It is made of woven loves
        and is lined with feathers
        of plum and cherry.

Buffalo

We are the great boulders of the American prairies.

We were the staff-of-life for the Plains Indians,
        the center of their world.

The white colonizing humans almost destroyed us.

Now we live behind fences,
        inoculated against disease,
        looked after by government rangers,
        our fur still prized for rugs.

We hang our heavy heads
        not only to eat sweet grasses
        but in the pain of knowing we are captives.

When the time comes that our last being vanishes,
        our shadows will remain the boulders
        of the American Plains.

We will welcome you to sit on our warm shadows.

Butterfly

My home is the rainbow.

I am the rainbow.

When I dance about the earth,
      I gather the colors of the flowers.

I go behind your eyes
      only to see beauty.

You are the rainbow
      and I love you.

Cat
—for Ruffn and Tumble and in memory of
Daffodil, Beast, Dustball and Yuki

Let me lament for you.

Give me your pain.

It is for me to cry your tears.

No one need know.

Your sadness is mine:
       it belongs to no one else.

I can hold your hurts here with me
       behind the mountain softness
       of my fur,
       behind the nightness
       of my eyes,
       deep behind the ins and outs
       of my claws.

It is in my alert soundlessness
       that I know you.

I purr to soothe your silence.

When I stare into the puzzling distance,
       I see a world you do not see.
       This is where I love you.

Let me lament for you.

Please. It is my duty, you know.

Caterpillar

Like you, I must change.

As much as I love wandering
      among petunias and apple blossoms,
      my roaming years are brief.

Unlike you, I know I will change
      into something beautiful
      though short-lived.

When you see me dreaming in a rose,
      remember beauty begins with wandering
      and is short-lived.

Cicada

Cloud

I change my shape
      to lizard or frog for rain.

I change my shape
      to buffalo or bear for power.

I change my shape
      to dancers for movement.

I change my shape
      to a multitude of trees
      for safety.

I change my shape
      to wings for flight.

I change my shape
      to a great plain of flowing colors
      for tomorrow.

When you look at me,
      I change my shape to your shape
      and invite you to join me in the sky.

Cow

If you allow us to live kindly
      in sweet grassy fields,
      we will teach you
      to be tender and humble
      on earth.

And when we give you our milk,
      we give you our patience,
      which is our strength.

We do not say much to you.

It is only when you see
      your reflection
      in our soothing eyes
      that you will know we love you.

Crab

I have eyes on stilts.

My two claws are as useful
        as your ten fingers.

I am my own house.

And when I dance
        from side to side,
        my ballet is the envy
        of fish and oysters.

Somewhere in the waters
        where I live,
        I have a hiding place
        where even the stars
        cannot find me.

Do you have a hiding place?

Cricket

In my season,
       in my season,
          my song is sharp like chips of stone.

Stones are my night and there I sing.

My blackness is my night. It is my song.

In my season,
       in my season,
          my song is bright like a red poppy
          in a great field of grass.

Fields are my homes and there I sing.

My brilliance is my day. It is my song.

I love the moon,
       who is my echo,
       who listens to my song.

And I love you,
       who listens to my song,
       who listens to my song,
       who listens to my song.

Please be my echo.

Deer

I carry the roundness of the moon
     in my horns.

It is my light in the darkness,
     sometimes full,
     sometimes hidden.

The coyote is my wind,
     my flute music
     in the mountain.
     He goes where I go.

The birds move with me.
     They lead me on my path
     in the mountains.
     They go by my side.

I carry the roundness of the sun
     in my horns.
     It is my light at dawn,
     sometimes warm,
     sometimes cool.

With the moon,
     with the coyote,
     the birds,
     the sun,
     I travel over the mountain
     in harmony.

Please come sit in my horns.

Dog

—In memory of my Dog Year friend
Tadao (Rio) Suzuki

When I take my walks,
I stop to listen to the voices
of the world.

When I pause,
I lie in shady places
to feel the movement of the planet.

When I open my mouth,
my tongue tastes the sweetness
and sourness of the world.

When I doze easily,
my ears open for you.
I have many things to tell you.

Sometimes,
sometimes when you touch me
with your soft voice and your strong,
kind hand, I think you understand.

I give you my loyalty and caring forever.

Even when you are angry and hurt me,
I remain your companion forever.

Even when you are loving and hurt me,
I remain your companion forever.

Elephant to Ladybug

The moonflower came with us.
It flowered and flourished unseen.

—Frances Hunter,
from "The Moonflower," *Sesame*

Elephant

Oh! We are the big Ones! The old Ones!

It is difficult for us to hide,
      even in the farthest jungles and valleys.

Humans have destroyed our lives.

They have forgotten
      we taught them how to write.

They have forgotten
      we taught them how to be gentle
      with one another
      and the creatures of the world.

One day, they will remember
      who we are
      when they remember
      who they are.

We want you to find a gentle place
      in your lifetime
      to remember.

Fantasy Creature
—for my Dragon Year daughter Jeni Kelleen

You may find us when clouds
    change into dragons.

You may see us in the colors of gardens
    or when oil on the highway
    becomes a phoenix.

You may discover us in the cracks
    and lines of old wooden boards
    on your walls,
    our eyes watching you.

And in the shadows under trees
    or next to stones in temples
    you may see unicorns, gorgons
    or lost gods.

You may smell us in the winds,
    hear our laughter
    or see our faces weeping
    across the valley in the cliff side.

We are the fantasy creatures
    who live in your imagination,
    emerging in your silent times.

You can give us to friends
    as your most treasured gift.

You can keep us to burn away your fevers.

Our wish is to be real to you.

Fireflies

After the first night
       when you saw the stars
       fade from the dawn sky
       we remained
            to remind you of the darkness.

Our brightness
       is your light too.
       It is brief and brilliant.
       It is shocking and recurring.

When we leave our summer-autumn
       world,
       it is as we entered it:
       full of beauty,
       full of wonder,
       growing and dying.

Will you leave your world
       as you entered it?

Fish

—in memory of my fantail goldfish Princess

I am the waters of the world.

My back is the mountain glacier
        and the wave.

Through my mouth move
        all the raindrops,
        all the seas,
        all the tears.

When your fingers touch me,
        life enters your heart.

You smile and your mouth
        becomes my shape.

I am always a smile.

Flower

Let me tell you
       where my sweet scents
       and bright colors come from.

My colors and sweet scents
       come from your heart
       as you look at me.

I only need you to look at me
       to become sweet-scented
       and radiant with color.

When you look at me,
       I blush
       because you recognize
       your own beauty.

Ah! You too are blushing.

Fly

I will buzz and buzz and buzz
     and make circles and circles and circles
     about your ears and face and eyes.

I will whoosh and whoosh and whoosh
     and make lines and lines and lines
     about your window and table and chair.

I will be silent for a second or two,
     long enough for you
     to see my antennae tasting the air
     so I can buzz and whoosh
     where you are.
     I enjoy the annoyance I cause you.

I am the child spirit
     that you were
     when you first waved your arms in the air.

Four Seasons

Spring sees you awakening,
        beginning songs
        for breaking shells
        with larks and nightingales
        and moves on.

Summer scents your body
        in your spiciness,
        your roseness,
        your marigoldness
        and moves on.

Autumn pauses, listens to you
        shaking and storing
        bits of your life for replanting
        and moves on.

Winter watches you capturing
        shadows in gardens
        of sand and stone
        and moves on.

Fox

I am not there where you look for me.

I am the many moods of you.

I am the smiling bite of you.

I am the soft teeth of you.

I am the sleeping alertness of you.

I am the Kabuki dance in you that does not move
    when dogs bark.

I am your fox.

I am your morning sun.
    I change from white to yellow
    to orange to red to no color.

Let us travel together,
    changing our colors,
    welcoming dawn.

Frog

We will hop and jump and plop
     and splash
     from early Spring into Summer
     and late Autumn, then go
     hopping and jumping and plopping
     and splashing
     into Winter
     when we will pause and rest
     and sleep with seeds.

There we will build new vigor
     for ourselves
     and for the world.

We will wait for the next Spring
     when the first rain
     will call us awake.

Then we will hop and jump and plop
     and splash
     from early Spring into Summer
     and late Autumn, then go
     hopping and jumping and plopping
     and splashing
     into Winter
     when we will pause and rest
     and sleep with seeds.

Fruit

There are festivals every day.

Above us, stars brighten our trails.
        They are our lanterns.

Below us, voices in the earth
        hum their songs.
        They are our instruments.

Beside us, shadows move to make masks
        across our faces.
        They are our dances.

In your orchard, trees smile blossoms.
        They are our costumes.

We are celebrating your ripening.

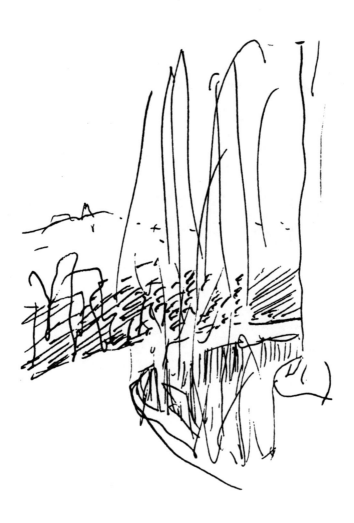

Grasshopper

I am the dancer in your feet
       as you move among grasses and stones.

The green of my body is your Spring.

The brown of my body is your Autumn.

I hum, hum when I dance.

In Winter I dream of Spring.

I am the dancer in your feet.

We move together between Spring and Autumn.

In Winter you and I will dream
       of Spring and hum, hum, hum.

Horse

—for my Horse Year daughter Jain Kellain

There is thunder in my hooves,
thunder, like two quartz stones
meeting to make lightning.

There is wind in my mane,
wind, like the breathing
in the tops of Spring pine trees.

There is turquoise, agate and
obsidian in my eyes,
jewels that catch the sun
of morning, the moon and stars
of night.

There is strength in my body,
strength of a desert mountain.

There is playfulness in my bones
that calls to the playfulness
in you so we might go running
across the earth together,
you becoming me,
me becoming you.

House

You are like the turtle
      and the hermit crab.

You know a house is necessary.

No matter if you live in a cave,
      an apartment, up a tree,
      under a cardboard box,
      you have a home.

I am your home.

This is where your heart belongs.

This is where you share your love.

Ladybug

I never did like the song
      you sang in school,
      sending me home to my children
      and a burning house.

I know it was a nursery rhyme
      but you forgot
      how I wanted to stay in the garden,
      to be covered with sweet pollen,
      to be seen by children
      who knew I was a bright red star
      in the morning light.

You can sing to me now,
      but make it a joyous song
      about my being the bright red star
      in the morning light.

Thank you.

Lion to Seal

A person, how tiring.
I think I would prefer to be a flower right now,
bright and opened petaled.

　　　　　　　　　　　　　　　—Dana Negev,
　　　　　　　　from "Two Hoodlums," *I Om The World*

Lion

I enjoy frightening you humans.

It is great fun to growl,
        to switch my tail from side to side.

You may never understand my bravery.

It is only when you can be a true warrior,
        as I am,
        that you will never fight
        one another again.

I have a big voice but a gentle heart.

I carry firelight in my claws
        to frighten the shadows away.

Lynx

Please do not think ill of me
      when I catch a rabbit.

I am a hunter, as were your ancestors.

If you could join me in the hunt,
      I would teach you
      to walk gently, softly,
      as if you were not stepping
      on the earth at all.

And I would train your ears
      to listen for stirrings
      as silent as feathers falling
      from a passing bird.

Monkey
—for my Monkey Year friend Julius Lee Prater

My life appears to be just a laugh to you.

I know enough
        to love my tree,
        my bit of earth,
        and what each
        gives to me.

I know no more.

I find my world so simple.

Perhaps that is why my life
        appears to be a laugh
        to you.

Mountain

If you watch the moon rise
  over my peaks and valleys,
  you will know that the moon
  is my gift to you.

Even if you are at sea,
  somewhere the moon
  has come up over a mountain
  to give its light to your path.

I will never hold the moon
  in my arms for long.

You must have its changing brightness
  for the darkness in your life.

Mountain Sheep
—for my Sheep Year poet-friend Frances Hunter

Like you, human,
       I have my memories.
       They are hidden
       in the curl of my horns.

My child days are gone:
       green grasses,
       sweet honey smells,
       flowers in cloudbursts,
       sounds of winds in the shade of trees,
       climbing rocky cliffs,
       migrating across mountains,
       sharing my mother's milk.

In the zoo where I live now,
       the child in me
       hears only my mother calling.

Do you hear my mother calling?

Please tell her I am here
       and have no voice to answer her.

Mouse

I am the small softness in the grass.

My voice is soft.

My body is soft.

I often watch you
       from the dust-balls in the corner
       of your kitchen.

If I frighten you,
       I am sorry.

I only want you to feel
       my soft, playful breathing.

Owl

I am the night.

My claws hold your wound-without-a-name.

My feathers hold a thousand eyes.

I see you in the darkness of my moonlight.

I know your silence.

I see you in the brightness of the day.

You cannot hear me flying.

I am your silence.

It is your wound in my claws.

Pigeon

I may see you
    when you do not see me.

I am suspicious of you.

I have been your messenger for generations.

I can navigate the earth.

My family was sacred to Aphrodite. Now you
    chase me from street corners.

You have hunted me, taken my feathers,
    eaten my family for ages.

Should my family become extinct,
    you will hear the echo
    of my whirring in the wind
    as it brushes against your ears.

Plant

Life and death.

Blooming, harvested, lying dormant.

Flowers and seeds
    are gifts
    of my cycle.

They are all good. I have learned
    to let them pass by,
    accepting each in their time.

I let them pass
    so that I may survive
    and grow, and grow.

Rabbit
—for my Rabbit Year friend Jack DiBenedetto

Watch for me just as the day
       begins to darken.

I will show you my light
       at dusk when the sun
       begins to return
       to other lands,
       to other creatures.

I love the darkening of the earth
       where I live.

I widen my eyes.

I expand my ears.

I lengthen my feet and travel
       easily with adventures into dawn.

Watch for my light.

Move with me. Our lanterns will bring
       the dawn more quickly.

The sun will reflect us together,
       throw our shadows
       upon the mountain

Rain

When I float across the sky,
       over the earth and oceans
       softly, hanging like a veil
       or a skein of long hair,
       I am the she-rain.
       I am fertility.

When I rush over the mountains,
       the deserts, along wave tips,
       bringing lightning, thunder,
       heavy clouds, and pounding the earth,
       I am the he-rain.
       I am fertility.

I give this fruitfulness to you,
       the gentleness of she-rain,
       the firmness of he-rain.

You must have both to be human.

Each is your strength.

Each is your weakness.

Road

I am here for your journeys.

You may choose the road paved
      with asphalt or cement,
      a cold, hard, well-traveled road.

You may choose the road crawling
      through trees and bushes,
      a lonely, peaceful, shadow-carpeted road.

You may choose the road running
      between fences and power lines,
      useful to farmers and engineers.

You may choose the road flowing
      across empty fields
      where cows and wild creatures roam.

One day late in life
      you may look back to roads
      you have traveled
      to find them
      littered with memories,
      broken dreams, lost hearts.

Sea

My coming in and going out
      is your pulse.

My ebb and flow
      is your breath.

When you sit with me
      there is peace,
      there is calm
      and there is storming
      and crashing.

I am your pulse and your breath.

I am your ebb and your flow.

Come sit with me.

Together we shall draw lines
      from one star to another
      and a circle about the moon
      and a circle about the sun.

Seal

My name is Seal.

My name tells you
I am a partner of the sea.

In my brown roundness,
      I can float on waves
      or dive deep
      where clams and kelp fill my ocean bed.

I would like to play with you,
      roll in the sand,
      jump off rocks into the surf,
      clap our flipper-hands together
      in seal games.

One day, you must come alone
      to the place I live.
      We will dream together
      and make friends of dolphins,
      otters, lobsters and whales.

Sea Shell
to
Who Walks
Beside You?

. . . all I have to do is choose, pick up a stone,
put it to my ear,
listen.

—Cynthia West,
from "Hearing What Is," *Rainbringer*

Sea Shell

I am the music in your ears.

I am the universe
      below the surface of the sea
      that is the song for you to sing.

I am your song
      secreted in the spiral
      created by the swirling of the sea.

When you listen to my song,
      you will hear the whisper of the clouds,
      you will hear the movement of the stars
      from night to day.

I am the hidden music of you.

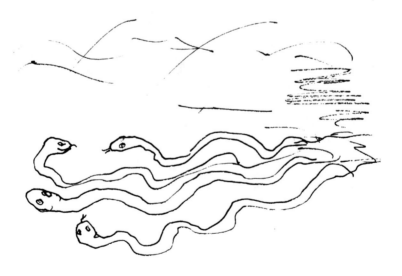

Snake

I am your fear.

I crawl about the earth
        trying to hide so you cannot find me.

I am your hate.

I try to hide from you
        in deep dark places.

My hiding is my cleverness.

My hiding is your darkness.

When you dance,
        I feel your movement.
        I feel your fear and hate.
        I carry them with me.

When you are most quiet
        I feel your warm blood.
        I carry your warmth with me.

I am your messenger to all things
        under the earth.

Spider

Have you seen my web in moonlight,
    circle upon circle upon circle
    of brightness?

Have you seen my web in sunlight,
    illuminated circles upon circles?

In the mornings when there is dew
    in the air, I weave upon the edges
    of crystals.

Start at the center of my woven labyrinth,
    use my threads to weave
    yourself a swallowtail of light,
    beginning here and ending there.

This will be your spirit garment
    so you may move in beauty
    where flowers bloom,
    where waters flow,
    where stones are still.

In the night, when there is prayer
    in the air, we will weave together
    on the edge of a star.

Squirrel
—for my squirrel Aphrodite

I know.

It is my tail that charms you.

It is my tail that attracts
the attention of birds and foxes.

I speak with my tail.

It is my laughter and my song.

And when I run up trees to store my food,
my tail polishes the air
and enlarges the smile on your face.

I flip my tail in joy.

Stone

Over there
          I am bathed in pools of watercress
          and thyme.

Over there
          I am carved and smoothed.
          My bird and animal and human
          is freed to greet you.

With your fingers
          you beautify me.

With your eyes
          you see me as the moon or sun.

With your ears
          you hear my silence.

With your nose
          you receive me in watercress
          and thyme.

With your mouth
          you give me your name.

Over here,
          under your feet,
          in your hand,
          against your back,
          above your head,
          I give you strength.

Tree

I stand for you upon the earth.

I am your arms and legs and your
        shadow under the soil.

I hold you as the young bird.
        I hold the snow of you
        in winter.

When you cry, I catch the rain
        of your tears to grow
        more strong.

When you speak, I catch your
        words to wave in the winds,
        to send your breath
        to all the stars.

Your sadness, I drop as leaves.

Your joys, I drop as leaves.

I stand for you upon the earth.

Turkey
—in memory of Cranberry,
Mayflower and Pumpkin

I am the fan-dancer of the bird world.

When I raise my feathers,
    I am beauty.

When I raise my feathers,
    I carry a rainbow around the world
    you walk on.

When I raise my feathers,
    I am blushing in brush-brown softness.

I will strut around you,
    asking you to spread your arms
    to make an invisible fan
    around your body
    and become as beautiful as I am.

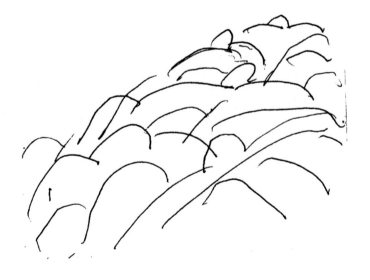

Turtle
—in memory of my terrapin turtle Patience

I am AH H H,
  round and firm.

My feet are EEE EEE,
  sharp and pointed,
  able to carry the AH H H
  from here to there.

AH H H   AH H H.

A mound of warm breath
  comes to AH H H you
  out of a long stretched neck
  from deep inside the dark cave,
  where my heart beats with your heart.

AH   AH   AH   AH   EEE   EEE.

Wind

Sit with me.
      Let me surround you.

I shall carry your cries and murmurs
      to become your voice
      for a thousand years.

I shall speak for you
      through masks of beaten gold,
      masks of carved wood and bone,
      masks covered with painted cloth.

I shall travel about the universe,
      entering pyramids and tipis,
      caves, openings behind stars
      and rusted bodies of ships.

I shall travel out of time.

I shall meet you on your return journey
      on your way home.

We shall talk together to awaken sleeping shadows
      in the dusty mirrors.

Wolf

False stories about me
        have kept you
        from learning from me.

Oh! I could teach you the power
        of loving your family.

Oh! I could teach you to know
        of winter storms and spring thaws.

Oh! I could teach you how
        to track passing deer and ghosts.

Oh! I could teach you to sing
        to the moon and stars,
        how to hear the songs
        the night sky returns to you
        when you listen with my ears.

Who Walks Beside You?
—in memory of my dogs Boy and Cokey

It is devotion that walks beside you.

My life is dependent upon you.

You can have love and beauty if
     you reach out your hand
     to say a word of praise to me.

I pass through your life,
     waiting for us to share
     peaceful adventures.

Let me touch you with my gentle paws,
     let me touch your face
     with the sweetness
     of my tongue.

I want to walk beside you.

I love you.

Notes about James McGrath

James McGrath, poet, visual artist and teacher, lives in La Cieneguilla, Santa Fe, New Mexico. He is known for his narrative poetry in the KAET/PBS American Indian Artist Film Series of the 1970s: *Charles Loloma, Allan Houser, R.C. Gorman, Helen Hardin, Lonewolf and Morning Flower,* and *Fritz Scholder.* His poems have been published in fifteen anthologies. His collections of poetry *At the Edgelessness of Light* and *Speaking With Magpies* are also published by Sunstone Press.

James was creative writing instructor at the Institute of American Indian Arts in Santa Fe in the early 1960s. He spent twenty years as the arts and humanities coordinator for the Department of Defense Overseas Schools in Europe and the Far East.

He was poet-artist in residence with the US Information Service, Arts America, in Yemen, Kingdom of Saudi Arabia, and in the Republic of the Congo in the 1990s.

James regularly attends the Listowel Writers Week in Listowel, County Kerry, Ireland, and has worked with Natalie Goldberg, Sharon Olds, David Whyte, Mark Doty, Marjorie Agosin, Alastair Reid, and Nuala Ni Dhomhnaill.

The title of this collection was inspired by Marjorie Agosin, poet, teacher, and human rights activist, who inscribed her book *Invisible Dreamer:* "To James McGrath A dreamer of invisible things."

MILLIE